40 feet down

dougie padilla

LUNA BRAVA PRESS
Northfield, MN

First Printing: 2024

ISBN 978-1-7330911-4-5

LUNA BRAVA PRESS
1210 Archibald Court
Northfield, Minnesota 55057

www.dougiepadillapoet.com

Cover photo: Dougie Padilla

Cover design: Pete Sandvik, Perfect Circle Creative

Publications manager and book design: Karen Wilcox

LUNA BRAVA PRESS
Northfield, MN

Books by dougie padilla
(www.dougiepadillapoet.com)

6 poems

*RUMP: 6 poems and a reprise on the first year of the dark reign
of the 45th president of the United States*

pepin diary

river town

*Lucky 70
(suerte)*

*diggin' on django
(dharma stories)*

40 feet down

for Hannah and Eli

"As a bee seeks nectar from all kinds of flowers, seek teachings everywhere.

Like a deer that finds a quiet place to graze, seek seclusion to digest all that you have gathered.

Like a madman beyond all limits, go wherever you please and live like a lion completely free of all fear."

- Dzogchen Tantra

contents

contents

contents

the antler men

1.

it's evening, the sun is growing old.
grown men, thirty of them,
dance down the street.
they are dancing towards me.
they are in their daily clothes,
in work shirts and suits,
in button-downs and flannels,
in lines, five across,
in lines ten rows deep.

and they are all holding deer antlers
up to their heads,
deer antlers,
four point, six point racks,
all dancing,
silently dancing,
their heads bobbing left and right,
all dancing towards me.

they are holding antlers to their heads,
they are dancing right towards me.

2.

there are prayers that no one else can sing.
there are prayers that no one else can know.

i live alone in this farmhouse now because i can.
i am not worried about finding my way
back thru the woods this winter.

on reading su tung po

(for natalie goldberg)

the weather is hotter than hades, as they say.

dougie sick as a dog with covid,
isolated, alone,
his wife far away
up north
near the cities.

old friends dying, dying.
even the guy across the street
last night.

and reading su tung po again,
banished once more,
this time to hainan province -

"how many exiles have ever returned?"

yet this hammock is remarkably soft,
the breeze is light and cool.

and now sunset wanders in towards me
here in the backyard
and i forget all my worries.

three non-haiku

dog snoring on the old couch
lake ice melting early
my wife lives too far away

~

herons slowly march the swamp
a chorus of chanting frogs
what has become of winter?

~

faint rainbow sundog
hanging over frozen lake
gone in a heart beat

the muskies

(for douglas josé)

well, actually, the muskies too.
i mean they don't really show up much either.
god knows how many times i've tossed a lure into a
lake/river/pond/stream/the cosmos,
waiting, always unsuccessfully, hour after hour
for that magnificent explosive strike,
their massive muscular bodies uncoiled,
my lure snatched and run towards deep water,
towards canada, towards the artic, towards a better life
somewhere across the globe, say in berlin,
with tasha and her young kids,
the lovely little park down the block,
nights we can always get a babysitter and
hit a club over in kreuzberg and pretend
we are young again just for a bit
and dance and drink way too much
and then uber it home and have hot sweaty sex
til way too late and then the kids wake us in bed early
even tho we have bad hangovers
and then it's time to go to church two streets over,
you can hear the bells ringing right now.

and getting a muskie into the boat isn't easy either,
i lost one right there as i lifted it from the water,
its powerful body suddenly, suddenly flapping hard
in my hands, and suddenly the hook loosened,

suddenly everybody's screaming and it's gone,
gone with a great embarrassing splash gone.

and now this poem is close to gone too

and i'm not sure i'll get it in the boat.
it's not exactly a muskie of a poem either,
more like a crappie or sunfish, small, but good eating,
sorta like the one douglas josé caught fishing with me
at silver lake from that bridge to the island
when he was, what was it, eight?

fernando

returning home from a few hours spent at the northfield
buddhist meditation center, sitting and then listening to
a talk by a dharma teacher from the cities, i somehow
fall into my computer and the internet and a site called
"fernandomania" and it is 1990 again and fernando
valenzuela is pitching his no hitter against the cards and i
am quietly weeping as he closes out the game and what a
wonderful moment that was too, for the dodgers, for base-
ball, for mexico, for me.

so then i find all sorts of videos about fernando, his life
and times, where he is now, the dodgers retiring his jer-
sey, and, most importantly, how he added the "screwball"
to his arsenal in the minors and how that changed his
game. so i think about how i can add a screwball to my ro-
tation, whether i have too many pitches already, too many
mediocre pitches, a decently slow fastball, a looping curve,
a change-up that is inadequate because of the aforemen-
tioned slow fastball, a slider that sometimes doesn't slide,
and the ace of my pitches, the knuckleball, which also
doesn't always work, cause no knuckleball always works.
so why add another pitch? but i'm more like thinking
"what's to lose?"

and, thus, i again wonder what ikkyu thought of dogen, of
what hafiz would say about dogen, or ikkyu for that mat-
ter. and then i wonder what james hillman would say if we
talked zen and emptiness and dharma and even fernan-
do and baseball. i know he woulda dug talking baseball
alongside zen. and i wish the wonderful anishnabe artist
jim denomie were here now. methinks hillman would en-
joy mixing it up with denomie, james woulda dug jim.

maybe i'll try dialing him up on the other side, see if i can get some input from the beyond. "dear mr. hillman, are you listening? dear brother man, how can a guy navigate dogen, ikkyu, hafiz and hillman and baseball inside the same story? is that even remotely possible? and what if i added a wild painter magician like jim denomie or like nikki st. phalle or a fierce feminist lobo poet like diane di prima, what would happen then? james, how do you think that would all shake out? i mean, i'll be listening for your response. make sure you get thru to me."

it's the middle of winter now.
the bottoms of my feet are often numb,
it's been that way for a few years.
i turn seventy-five soon,
how did that happen?

odd numbers have a tinny sound

1.

i just told my wife
that odd numbers have a tinny sound.
and that even numbers feel
like soft bark
or moss.

i also said i love the numbers
48 and 52.
cause if you add 2 to 48
or subtract 2 from 52
you have 50.
for both.

i find that attractive.
comfortable.

she thinks i'm nuts.

2.

have you noticed that nothing,
i mean nothing,
has an edge.
everything is one
with the space that surrounds it.
the mind just makes up
the notion of boundary.
edge is a perceptual invention,
like harmony
or complimentary colors.

3.

and, my love,
i swear
i can find no line
where you start
and i end,
where i end
and you start.

that's all just made up
and handed to us as kids.
really, it's all just one big soup.
that's what love is,

soup.

dogs of war

last night the dog woke susan at one in the morning cause
she desperately had to go outside and drink water out of
the bird bath and maybe barf somewhere or maybe shit
watery shit cause yesterday was stella's make-believe
birthday (we don't actually know when she was born
cause she was a rescue, running wild in southern indiana,
probably turned loose cause that's what happens with
coonhounds that don't hunt) - anyway, we spoiled her all
day, gave her a way too big a bone and some dog bakery
treats with doggie birthday treat icing on them, all this
on top of her daily evening dry dog food/wet dog food/
raw egg dinner and obviously it was too much, but that's
how we roll, dog spoilers that we are and i didn't wake
cause i was deep asleep downstairs, buried in my under-
ground sleep cave basement hideaway as i need to bury
myself way down, alone, into the ground in order to get
a good night's sleep, the kind with dreams and rest and
answers and even a hint of delight where all the cher-
ries line up once you pull the handle and wait and watch
the machine roll cause you may never be back to reno
again or, even better, vegas, where you can spot showgirls
walking around town on their way to the 7-11, which is
kinda like gods dropping in from a different planet cause
they're sooo tall and dressed up, made up fancy, even in
high heels tho it's just a trip to the grocery store, (and are
they boys or girls or do we even care?), but what other
godz are there these days, godz that walk among us? but
i was young and easily impressed by all things sexual and
female and mythical back then, back in the reno days, my
mind like hansel and gretal and the witch wanting to stuff
all us young 'uns into the stove and bake us for dinner,
which is a strange place for me to go with this one, but, on

the other hand today's gonna be a good day cause the
swelling around my pulled tooth has gone down and
there's less blood underneath my new retainer and my
headache is almost gone what with all the tylenol and
advil and acupuncture and yoga and the ground is white
with snow again, three days in a row, tho it's almost mid-
april and shouldn't winter be gone now and shouldn't we
be rounding the bend to spring at last? god, i had a whole
night spent dreaming about green last night, green grass
literally everywhere in that dream and now squirrels out
my back window hop around happily, madly chasing after
each other across the snow and i can't get rid of the image
of ukrainian soldiers, stinger missiles on their shoulders
facing down russian tanks, blown up vehicles everywhere,
bodies strewn across the sidewalks, cold gray winter days
reigning still in that part of the world too, maybe cold gray
winter days there for a long time to come, maybe forever
for some of those folks, god bless them. and may the man
that loosed his dogs of war on these people rot in hell,
soon i hope.

step into the dream

(for andy maus)

dreamt all night that the bear would come back so
i could follow him into the woods.

dreamt that the woods were made of cashmere and down.

then, took steps this morning to trade in my truck
for canvas and brushes and oil paints, mostly blues,
some reds, one tube of green, another of black.
who needs a truck anyways?

plus, the woods are still there, right alongside the road.
the bear is still there, in the woods.
the canvas remains unpainted.

step into the dream.

koan

the world we frequent
is comprised of surfaces.

don't be fooled.

heading for juarez

the orishas told me to go, i swear.
well, the ones that will still talk to me.
i heard from the large birds also,
the eagles, the vultures,
the occasional oversize crow.
they always chat in my ear,
chat until i go half nuts.

plus, i threw the tarot on my iphone
(i bought a cheap app).
it said: "the world" card,
followed by "the hanged man",
then "the hermit",
then "the emperor"
(best to retreat a bit and face this
with all yr inner talents).

so now i simply wait, wait to hear
from my favorite cousin's son,
wait to hear from across the border,
from la familia, from the cousins,
from the past that's fast disappearing.

hell, i wait to hear
from the other side too,
from ventura parked in paradise,
in a lovely green meadow
overlooking a lovely blue lake,
sitting there with his mother elvira,
with his uncle gabino,
with his abuelo gabino, his aunt pilar,

sitting there with my dad,
donald gabino.
god they loved each other.

so will his son, ventura junior,
get married this winter?
will he send me an invite?
will i find out more than a week
ahead of the big event, will i
have time to get there?
(it's a honkin' 24-hour drive
from minnesota to chihuahua!)

sometimes the difficult thing
about being norwegian/mexican
is that the difference
between tortillas and lefse,
(tho marginal visually),

can be the distance

from the sierra madre

to sognefjord.

it's four below out there

it's four below out there,
cold as crap.
i was up half the night with back pain,
too much back pain.
so i got up and sat in my chair,
talked to the spirit world a while.
that was helpful.

i want to talk about angels now.
i'm tired of talking about demons
and crazies and hungry ghosts
(there are so honkin' many).
anyways, at 70 years old,
angels are the more interesting subject.

let's start by looking at the sides of things.
everything has a side within a side.
and a side to that.
to see thru something
you must look from the side.
and you must feel with your looking.

for example, a sunset might look
just like a sunset to most folks,
but from the side it's closer
to the halleluiah chorus
in multiple dimensions,
more like an orgasm.

but the kind of orgasm
like when you're twenty-six
and living in a commune

and you've been picking blackberries
on a hot summer's day
in the meadow next to the back woods
and you're all sweaty and tired
and you've filled your mouth
with the most beautiful
plump and voluptuous wild
wisconsin blackberries
and you close your eyes
and concentrate
and begin to chew
and your whole being explodes
into a wealth of taste and sensation
and glory and love and wildness
and for that exact moment
life is full and good and beautiful
and o god so much so much
and yes let's go on with it forever,
let's go on with it forever,
yes, let's go on with it forever...

an angel is pretty much like that.
only without the orgasm part,
or the berry thing,
or the part about sides
and sunsets.

with angels less is more,
where more means
everything.

god bless all those that walk in the light.
god bless all those that walk
without the benefit of the light.
god bless all those that carry others,

that hold their hand,
that feed them,
that dress their wounds.
and especially,
god bless those
that are embodied
for just this short while.
may they live in the understanding
that living isn't everything,
that it is actually just a small thing,

though it is everything.

nixon and reagan

fifteen below isn't that bad if you grew up
with thirty below and a paper route.
but that's like saying that trump ain't so bad
cause you made it thru nixon and reagan.

a short dissertation on the knuckleball

("a knuckleball or knuckler is a baseball pitch thrown to
minimize the spin of the ball in flight, causing an erratic,
unpredictable motion.")

to aspire to knuckleball wisdom:

1) learn long, hard, and well. this is not an easily mastered
way to the majors, much less a way to stay there.

2) throw it slow. unlike the rest of life out there,
the ball needs slow. don't get riled up, pumped up,
energized. stay cool.

3) don't let the ball spin. if it doesn't spin, it has a life
of its own. you can't predict what it will do, nobody
can. let it work its magic.

4) piss off your opponent, make him look pathetic. thus,
make enemies for life. that doesn't matter, it's just a game.

5) piss off your teammates. especially the catchers
who mostly can't catch the pitch. and, of course, your
opponents do hit alot of homers off you when the knuck-
leball just doesn't work, which thus pisses off your team-
mates. c'est la vie.

6) last a long time. like ten years longer than like anybody
else, cause it's an old man's pitch, it doesn't waste your
body, doesn't waste your mind. thus, knucklers have more
fun. and spit on the graves of their compatriots.

7) go into the hall of fame in relatively good shape.
(see number 6)

8) retire to florida by 45 with your third wife and a good-looking sailboat in the keys.

so call it the knuckler, the flutterball, the bug, the floater, the dancer, the butterfly, the ghostball, call it what you want, i've been called all of those myself... and a whole lot more. but with these gorgeous caribbean skies and my boat in lovely shape, i don't much care what they called me back in the day, back in the bigs.

tho i am thinking of running hashish into the states for a bit of excitement.

can't be any harm in that, eh?

far from the capitol

clanging and banging, another train
pushes hard thru town
as i read su tung po here at a picnic table
alongside this great gray river.

i am growing old now, even as
thirty or so strikingly white seagulls
tilt and turn and sail
over these perpetual waves.

su tung po would be at peace
in this place, far from the capitol,
far from the mandarins
and the courtyards of power.
sometimes, i too am at peace here.

later today i will go to the dollar store
and see if they have any hand sanitizer in yet,
they've been out for weeks.
you can't be too careful with the virus,
tho sitting alone in my backyard all summer
in this small wisconsin village
has been pretty effective.

another three non-haiku

seven days in the studio
time to head home
i miss my dog

~

the squirrel sprinting
across the phone wire
has no thoughts of death

~

robin guarding her nest
attacks my head
like jordan attacking the basket.

goat back hill

the stars tonight are bigger and brighter than all of goat
back hill, bigger and brighter than all the prophecies of
samuel in the temple, bigger and brighter than when
gautama budhha sat under the bodhi tree at bodh gaya,
bigger and brighter than the knicks the year they had
earl the "pearl" monroe and won the whole damn thing.
so maybe tonight, say after midnight, if the clouds settle
down into the soybeans, if the fullish blue moon rises
from the new corn, if said moon also rises early enuf from
its home over by wabasha, if all the planets align and you
and i are not too tired, too lazy, too old, if we haven't had
too many glasses of pinot grigio at the new wine bar down
the block, if we're not too loutish and shallow and dim, if
jesus doesn't come down from the cross and address us
personally (and please not in greek or aramaic or latin or
sanskrit), if coltrane doesn't pick the night for a repeat
performance of his concert at the guthrie theater, the
one i saw in the summer of '65 when i was a jazz fanatic
callow youth and he played "my favorite things" on the
soprano sax, if the mississippi river doesn't part down the
middle and bud grant or dennis green leads the vikings
and their faithful from the football hinterlands into green
bay's lambeau field and brings home an nfc north title, if
god doesn't constantly harmonize with herself/himself
like the throat singers of the khalkha people of western
mongolia or turn grains of silica into deep blue mystical
stained glass windows like the ones chagall created that
dwell now at the abbell synagogue in jerusalem...

if, if, if...

well, then my hands just might morph into golden mari-
posas and fly away, mi amigo, fly south, and my ears might
turn into ears of harvest corn and feed the wandering deer,
my belly might attain true and lasting redemption after a
pizza from basil's down on water street, sausage and green
pepper and onion and mushroom with red peppers, my
knees might dance again, at last, and there will be no
reggae, no salsa, no tango that is safe from me and from
whatever partner i choose from the cosmic sidelines and
my mind will drift then across these foggy fields out across
the lake into the darkness and then off to wherever minds
go when we unleash them and who cares if i am lost in
ecstasy again and if my body will be found weeks later on
a beach in goa, obvious evidence that i partied way too
hard, dancing all night on the beach with some beauty
many decades younger than me, my mouth wrangled into
a permanent smile, this soul simultaneously one with the
universe and sitting out the next dance, just one dance, all
this carrying forward on the next plane two heavens up
and one to the south of here.

this is not the time for grieving,

this is the time for joy.

let's take a moment here for bobby blue bland

once upon a time i was sitting with martín in a coffee
shop in south minneapolis, a lesbian hang-out mostly
(which i only point out cause, as a medicine man, he
thought it was quite amusing, a separate hang-out for
the lesbians) and then he was pointing out the ghosts in
the room, seems some folks aren't quite flesh and blood,
some folks are both alot less and alot more than that,
which makes the game all the more confusing for those of
us not so adept at the astral realms, those of us deep-
ly in need of a flesh and blood and bone world. which
brings up bobby blue bland, who i always associate
with chicago, but who was actually a memphis man, and
now he resides at memorial park cemetery, 5668 poplar
avenue, memphis, least his body has since the "lion of the
blues" departed for the far shores in 2013, tho i still hear
my fave "ain't no love in the heart of the city" in my head
all the time, especially when i'm painting in the studio
or especially now that today my wonderful wife is trying
to save a lost soul buried under a mountain of blankets
at the bus stop in the city in this winter minnesota cold,
the poor guy unable to talk at all this morning and when
can we get him to a shelter and do we even have room in
the shelters any more in this very hopefully post-trump
world?

no hippies

passing thru big sur
on highway 1 in '67,
on my way north to san francisco
and the "summer of love",
paused at a roadside cafe to pee
and saw this sign
nailed next to the front door:

NO HIPPIES
NO DOGS
NO MEXICANS

me, a wandering hippie,
a mexican-american,
and hitch-hiking cross country
with my dog.

precisely the target audience, i guess.

cowboy sez

(for gary snyder)

cowboy sez i can put an rv on his land up on top of the
bluffs, up there almost to lund, up there right after the
turnoff by sabylund church. he said he's got an 80 for
hay for his horses there. maybe there's some woods
alongside his farmland too, something for shade and
cover from road eyes, that would be nice, i could hide
out there. listen to the birds in the morning, the coyotes
at night. maybe i can get me a 26-foot trailer that a covid
camper sells off cheap when he loses his lust for the
great scenic outdoors, once he can hit the bars and clubs
in the city regularly again.

cause there's nothing like raindrops on the roof of
an aluminum trailer, especially a shiny silver zaftig
"airstream" from the fifties. and nothing like sitting out
the big weather in such a trailer in some lonely spot
where the wind can have a real go at you, can pick you
up and throw you at the stars or into the next county
over. talk about a way to face yr fears. one fall long, long
ago, the ex and i sat out some pretty stiff straight-line
winds in one such baby. we sat in the dark as the
trailer jumped and heaved and sang and retold the
whole wizard of oz story cause we were living on a short
rise on the very flat prairie out by paynesville, stearns
county, over in minnesota.

and now instead of fixing myself lunch i'm eating a
caramel apple i bought at the corner store near the
vineyard. god, it's wonderful. you know the kind of
caramel apple that has peanuts on the outside like at the

state fair back in the 60's. someday when the virus is just a memory i'll go to the state fair again, go early in the morning on senior's day before the throngs get there, go to the ag barns and look at the piles of very shiny apples, look at the very slimy newborn goats, listen to a whole barn of crazy honkin' roosters, check out the wildass postmodern seed art that the youngster artists have been concocting. then around noon i'll head down to the midway. right about then the millennials would be rising from their coffins and wandering over to the thrill rides, excited to be once again slingshotted into the heavens and then rebounded fast and hard just shy of the hard packed earth and then back into the skies again and then back almost to the hard ground again, each time ranging a little less far, finally setting into the whole notion of gravity and this planet as home. i have great admiration for these young wacko warriors who i generally berate. i could never ride the slingshot. i will never ride the slingshot.

and i forgot to ask cowboy if he likes the cowboys, tho i'm pretty sure he's a packers fan. and i wonder if he prefers theravada buddhism to zen. maybe he's more of a krishna devotee. i'm wondering what his pronouns are. i shouldn't just presume because he's a cowboy and a carpenter that he's self-identifies as male. i wonder how oscar wilde self-identified. how diane di prima self-identified. how james dean self-identified. hell, how krishna self-identifies. these are confusing times. identity used to be much easier. easier used to be easier.

and now i'm thinking that cowboy only likes me because i tell long, confusing, and totally inaccurate stories. sometimes, he tells stories too. and i think he might also have a tendency to fib. hemingway exaggerated grossly. same with edna st. vincent millay. rilke, well, he was always desperate for depth, no matter the price. ikkyu pretty much didn't care what he said as long as it all had the stink of awakening about it. meanwhile, i'm not sure if postmodernists have much sense of awakening. i figure what with all their time spent deconstructing and, then, the inescapable reconstructing, there's not much time and space left for stillness and emptiness and inevitable delight. which reminds me of how dogen talked about "suchness". and that snyder talked about dogen talking about suchness. and now here i am i'm talking about snyder talking about dogen talking about suchness. such is the nature of this moment. such is the nature of suchness.

on being both an artist and a poet

being both an artist and a poet

is like having a doorknob for your left hand
and a boat sail for the right.

it's like singing in danish, yet composing in tagalog.

it's like having han shan in center field,
with nevelson starting at quarterback.

like having nureyev write the screenplay,
with lucille ball dancing the lead
and marc chagall directing.

the left-hand path*

my wife seems to think
that if she lets me go off
completely on my own
i'd most likely go feral,

me lost down along the river
in my storefront studio,
not bathing, sometimes,
for a week or more,

letting the dishes pile up,
rarely brooming,
never vacuuming,
a fair share of spiders
reaching from the corners
of the ceiling
out to wherever
their imaginations can ponder.

++++++++

the "left hand path" is difficult
for strangers to fathom.
from the outside it looks like
a series of random mistakes,
swirling in no particular order,
tasty yet confusing.

from the inside tho, it's
both better and worse,
stacks of minutes, hours, days,
thrown on the studio floor
in no particular way,

44

in no particular order,
rising when the sun rises,
setting when the moon sets.

dougie sez:

no need to soar above the warp and woof here,
no need to sit alone and challenge the heavens.

there is a point at which
all this comes together,
a point at which the gardens
release their fragrances,
a point at which we are lost
and alone in the beauty.

this is all about the light inside the light.

please take note.

* "Vamacara is a sanskrit term meaning 'left-handed attain-
ment' and is synonymous with left-hand path or left-path
(sanskrit: *vāmamārga*). It is used to describe a particular
mode of worship or spiritual practice (sanskrit: *sadhana*)
that is not only heterodox (sanskrit: *nāstika*) to standard
vedic injunction, but extreme in comparison to prevailing
cultural norms. These practices are often generally consid-
ered to be tantric in orientation."

- Wikipedia

love nest heaven

the winter of '69
susan hagen and i lived
up burntside mountain in b.c.
in a cabin with michael kaplan,
our med school buddy from
the forest street commune,
back in palo alto hippie days
(he's the one that kept an
african lion cub in the backyard).
holed up thru the mountain cold,
we pretty much only ate brown rice,
a bit of halvah somebody sent us,
and all the bear meat we could handle,
meat that a neighbor gave michael
for skinning his trophy shot,
that expensive stanford med school
education put to good use at last.
occasionally, we would get our hands
on an orange or two to stave off scurvy.
you can't be too careful.

that spring, susan and i
came down off the mountain,
down mountain four miles by atv
to the nearest thing that passed for a road
and then on into the outskirts of vancouver,
to michael's sister's place at the ocean's edge.

once there, susan met jack, an ex-hells angel,
and bang, like lightening, they were gone,
gone down the coast road to san francisco
and, then, bang they were gone again

off to taos and the high mesa.
i didn't see her lovely face again for years.

heartbroke, i holed up across the street,
me the only american long hair
in that canadian commune utopia.
and since there were no rooms in the inn,
i found a coal bin in the basement,
cleaned it out damn good, painted it,
and moved in with my dog yase,
who promptly decided to have a litter
smack dab on my lap,
me gobstruck in awe
of the great birth miracle,
sticky, gooey dog placenta everywhere,
tiny pups rocking at their mama's teats
suckling their way back to milky bliss.

and then, just a few weeks later
as some kind of second breath of sweetness,
some kind of god given heavenly consolation
for all my aching, young man lost love pain,
my lost in the commune cellar despair,
a luscious and delightful young hippie girl
(o god what was her name?)
yes, a luscious young hippie sweetie appeared

all draped in buckskin and cowboy boots,
leather fringe hanging pretty much everywhere,
the prettiest pink silk camisole
and panties hidden beneath,
her smell so sweet,
so lovely.

god she fucked me senseless,

us stoned
and high as a kite

in that coal bin
love nest

heaven.

forty feet down

in the little town
along the big river lake
where I seem to spend
whole great chunks of my life,
mike the bartender at the bear's den
tells us stories of the lake floor bottom,
of his quiet life forty feet down,
of hours on end underwater,
life spent in solid sweet darkness,
unable to see his hands
at the end of his arms,
breathing thru a tube,
breathing slowly,
scooping clams
up out of the muck,
hoisting them up to the boat
and sending them off
to sushi stars
in tokyo, paris, and scottsdale –
or button makers
lost in pennsylvania hamlets.

we are all forty feet down, my friend.

plenty of work to do.
you can rest tomorrow.

something came down to me

(for margarita padilla torres)

and then, when i awoke, i knew
i had to search
for my great-grandmother,
lost from me as she is,
no photos, no stories,
lost to the family,
lost to mexico, to chihuahua,
lost to the old days.

and then, abruptly, i saw her,
i saw her over there,
she was on the other side,
just for a moment,
right there at the edge.

she was older than i had imagined,
her hair was grayer, shorter too.
she was sitting just outside the church,
the one on the other side of the village,
out beyond most of the houses,
out near the old adobe school,
the old one, the one that's mostly
falling down.

there was a small stream close by.
near where she sat there were cactuses.
and dogs, i remember the dogs,
three or four of them,
all black with white spots,
or white with black spots.

and right then, just when i saw her,
i knew that there was a bridge nearby,
a bridge across the stream,
tho i didn't actually see that bridge.

and there were birds crying out, loudly,
ravens, sparrows, blue jays, grackles,
tho i didn't hear those birds,
didn't actually hear those birds.

and i knew i had to leave
and come back later,
tho i wasn't sure when later was
or even what the way back might be,

but, i knew i needed to talk to her,
needed to talk to her despite all the years,
all the decades, needed to talk across
the dry chihuahuan desert,
across the border, across the states,
the states of the usa, of mexico,
across the desert.

and just then something came to me,
something that i cannot talk about,
something that i cannot touch,
something came to me.

and that something walked past me,
walked right past me late at night.
and that something was singing ever so quietly,
walking past me with the lightest of steps,
walking past and singing as if
i wasn't there, as if i wasn't at all.

and yes, i know now.
something came down to me
something that i cannot talk about,
something that i cannot touch.
something came down to me.

when is water fire?

1.

so my question to the taoist was:

"when is water fire"?

2.

and why do some buddhists insist on non-dualism?
don't they get bored?

non-dualism = dualism = non-dualism, etc., etc.

i say try skipping the thinking thing.
or maybe dance a bit,
touch the stars.

3.

i dreamed this morning of a long, muscled muskie
curled up in a red and white plastic picnic cooler,
covered with just enough water to survive.

4.

but why do poets rarely write about fish?

coyotes sometimes. bears maybe. horses, yes.
but fish?

mostly never.

in cat world

(for doug, annie's cat)

in cat world there are no dishes to wash, no clothes to fold, no truck to fill with gas for the trip south along the river tomorrow. in cat world there is no sense listening to johnny cash or the supremes or the clash or even gangsta rap, if yr into that kinda thing. and in cat world there are no zoom meetings. in cat world the kwik mart is irrelevent. in cat world having your burger without onions wouldn't even come up.

and remember, in cat world an endless sunbeam on a winter morning is the complete ballgame, the whole enchilada, the answer to every prayer.

just a sunbeam.

think about it.

at seventy-two

broken toes ache this morning as i wake,
as i struggle getting out of bed.

golden sunlight lies on the snow
outside my window.

this is not the life i had planned.

la oración (the prayer)

the air conditioner drones on in the background.
the gnats have their way with my hair.
overweight tourists parade
down main street to the lake.
the morning grows quieter and quieter,
slowly emptier, slowly more filled with grace,
more graceful.

today will be the day that the entire
world comes to my door and asks forgiveness.
today i will rest from my work carving linoleum blocks
into sea serpents and portraits of bank presidents.
today i will take the time to bless each and every
sentient being on this block, in this neighborhood,
in this county, on this whole planet,
each and every one:

may all those that traverse this veil of tears
find true peace in each and every sparkling moment,
even when that is not remotely possible.

may all those that dance thru this ever flowering
sphere of utter joy know the humanness of regret,
even as they sing ever closer to the sweetness
that sits inside this one true and sparkling moment.

may each and every one of us sleep well tonight,
sleep away the aches and pains of everyday life
in this utterly everyday place we try to call home.

and may each of us also not sleep at all
as long as young children cry all night

for their missing mothers,
lying alone on concrete detention center floors,
inserted along the border
with our good neighbors
to the south.

fargo song*

(for schnauzer)

i swear i love you big
as that building in fargo,
the big one all the way downtown,
just past the old bus station,
over there towards the river
that floods every year.
the river that floods every year.

god, maybe i love you even more,
maybe i love you more than more.
four days gone i'm such a mess,
four days home, i'm such a mess,
god, maybe i love you even more,
maybe i love you just more
than more than more
than more.

and i swear i love you as far as hopkins,
girls with raspberries in their hair,
all beehive hairdos high atop their heads,
the streets blocked off for the big parade,
and the beach boys turned up nice and loud.
the beach boys turned up nice and loud.

god, maybe i love you even more,
maybe i love you more than more.
four days gone i'm such a mess,
four days home, i'm such a mess,
god, maybe i love you even more,

maybe i love you just more
than more than more
than more.

and i swear i love you loud
as the crickets back by the shed,
over by the coulee creek,
across from the county road,
loud as you know they can be.
and they don't stop singing til morning.
the crickets don't stop singing til morning.

god, maybe i love you even more,
maybe i love you more than more.
four days gone i'm such a mess,
four days home, i'm such a mess,
god, maybe i love you even more,
maybe i love you just more
than more than more
than more.

* music by big davie ballman and the spoontones

this morning my hands are made of light

this morning my hands are made of light.
light that scatters off into the arroyos,
light that seems to wind across the mesas,
light that holds children closely in its arms,
light that we can't quite see from this far south,
light that passes thru angels.

and angels, sorry to speak of angels again,
but angels are pretty much a constant now
that i live marooned inside mi casa, so tiny,
so sparse, down here near where the creek finds
its way eventually to the rio grande gorge
and the stories we told down by its wild
raging waters way last spring, the virus
unchecked then, the virus also raging
now amongst la gente.

i am growing old still, even as we speak.
they have told me to stay inside,
but my spanish is bad and now
my english is worse
and all i can see is the music
and all i can hear are the drawings
and i have no food.
and i am out of ink, out of chalk,
out of crayons.

tho i am quite surely alive.

alive, yes, tho my knuckles are red
and frozen from the arthritis,
my knees are starting to buckle under the load,

i am losing my vision,
salt tastes like pepper.

so i am passing on my knowledge of water,
i am passing water thru my hands, passing
my hands through angels, passing
my hands thru angels.

this morning my hands are made of light.
and light is water.

i believe in dogs

i believe in dogs, not dogs that run for congress or dogs
that have a larger vocabulary than me, but dogs that will
sit thru a ball game, have a beer and a pretzel and then
later discuss camus by the fire. even dogs that can consider
max ernst's work, the later stuff. we're talking labs here
mostly.

and i believe in a nice pinot noir, something deep and sexy
enough to assuage my fears of not having rocked my day
to the max, not having changed the art world forever. we
don't have to get crazy here, something mid-range will do,
say fifteen or twenty bucks, something from the grocery
store, something to help me make it through sunset and on
to bed in time for sleep or, at least, sleep's first cousin.

and finally, i believe in my father who has been gone 28
years now, not counting the endless spaces between years,
once they're stood on end and numbered back-to-back. i
mean, sure, the man had his faults, but my god he had to
ride the rails and box his way thru small town
depression-era iowa just to eat whatever fried meat
and potatoes he could find.

mezcal

"mezcal, not to be confused with mescaline."
    - wikipedia, the free encyclopedia

o god, i think it would be pretty hard to confuse these two,
what with their different lifestyles, different voyages,
different muses, different goddesses.

maybe if i were lost in some sierra madre hole in the wall
cantina one winter with ted for a way too long-lost weekend
or month or year, maybe then, just maybe. but probably not.
no, probably not.

as i said, different goddesses.

a consideration of yves klein

i was making art last night in my sleep,
in my half-sleep too.

i was seeing hanging fields of marble blue
bird house constructions, all apartment buildings
with multiple unit architecture,
with multiple bird holes and perches,
all hung upside down overhead,
by cable sometimes, by fishing line,
some installations hanging from the ceiling,
some hanging from the trees.

in my dreamtime i was working out different
price structures for selling the art,
a standard base price for the work,
a sliding scale that slides up for the rich
and down for the poor,
so that everyone is charged the same,
more or less.

now, it's important that i get the color right for you.
it's so hard to describe color with words, even poetry,
kinda like opening a door with your elbows as they say.

online the color blue that matched is called 6666FF,
which is interesting cause 6 is by far my fave number.
the F thing is a bit disconcerting cause like many
of my generation the sight of an F on my report card
was scary, with ramifications on the home front.
still a bit upsetting it appears.

elsewhere, i found it described as "moderate blue",
with a hex triplet of #0087BD
and an HSV of 197°, 100%, 74%.
how strange the science of color appears to be.

i much prefer the thought of "chagall blue",
seemingly born out of a lifetime of standing
in front of an easel dreaming of a past life with bella,
although "international klein blue" was created
by the rather insane yves klein after
mountains of research to get the color
exactly, precisely right,

tho some think it happened
in that astounding moment
he dove off a building in a paris suburb,
his great "leap into the void"
back in the fall of 1960

also an invention
it seems.

poem written on my iphone in bed
immediately after kinda waking

the problem is that the poems sit at the bottom
of the lake and i have to dive for them.
and it's muddy cloudy down there.
and i don't last that long before i have to shoot
back to the surface for thank god more air.

plus, some days there's whitecaps on the surface
of the water so that isn't exactly helpful either,
pretty easy to gulp down some nasty river water
when you come back up too fast.

and diving for poems in the winter is almost impossible.
you chop a hole in the ice, then climb into a wetsuit,
put flippers on your feet, glove your hands,
and mask your face.

then you put on a weight belt, hold on to a rope and jump in,
sinking down fast to the cold, black bottom,
maybe thirty feet below, and praying that there's
enough light to see your new world,
praying that your breath will last,
praying that you will make it back
to the surface alive.

but looking up from the river's floor...
o god, it's all so gorgeous...

and there really is nothing better, ever,
than racing back to the upper world, poem in hand,

that first gasp of air re-inflating your lungs,
re-igniting life in your veins,

re-igniting your entire body,
driving waves of surprise thru
your whole being

after the poem has pulled you
down into those frozen, numbing
watery depths
for way, way too long.

rumi is more of a jabber

yesterday, back in my studio,
robert and coleman
debated rumi on youtube
while I painted a self portrait
with eyes all over my head,
eyes reaching out like the limbs of a tree,
eyes staring back at me constantly.

ok, rumi and hafiz in a cage match –
who comes out alive?

(technically, I don't think it's a debate
when both sides agree.)

my money is on hafiz
and his longer, stronger punches,
knockout punches.

rumi is more of a jabber,
he looks for openings
and then inflicts
whatever sharp awakenings he can.

inside my hands

inside my hands, there is no longer any arthritis,
no lousy tv sitcoms, no bad vegan hot dogs, no
bikers thinking they're god's gift to this corny
little tourist town, no ugly shopping malls erected
in third tier suburbs in the seventies.

inside my hands, major league baseball is playing
again and the twins are still in first place and all
of us are looking forward to a world series with
the dodgers in october instead of more virus and
endless zoom meetings morning after morning.

and inside my hands, i am having conversations with
willie mays, marc chagall, cher, and li po. we are
all enjoying a lovely summer day out on the lake on
my new pontoon boat. li po has asked for beer. i try
and appease him with a miller lite to no avail. he
says miller lite is not beer. chagall and willie mays
are arguing about frenchie post-structuralism, so i
try and steer away from them. cher and i are hoping
the fish will bite, we're fishing for walleye, but we'll
settle for anything, even catfish, tho they're hard
to clean.

tiffany bottoms

walking the dog in tiffany bottoms. and yes, i know that
sounds like a porn star name, but it's actually a huge wild-
life refuge. dog loves it here. dougie loves it here. probably
porn stars love it here. and it rained hard the last couple
days, the ferns are still growing strong even though it's
halfway through september. today they're still double
green bright green real green, green green. and i'm still
going pretty strong, even though i'm probably halfway
through september too, or probably more like halfway
through october. i guess it all depends on what your
definition of going strong is. picasso went forever, but
he was a major asshole. i wonder if that's what kept him
going strong. maybe there's something about just putting
your head down and pushing forward hard, everything
else, everyone else be damned, that keeps you alive and
pretty much forever rocking. meanwhile, i might mention
that some folks are not pushing forward hard. this year as
ever the twins suck the wild sucks the timberwolves suck
and of course the vikings kind of suck, tho the lynx and
the loons are winning some, sorta. and yes, i know that
intellectuals and poets and artists aren't supposed to be
into sports, but willie mays and mickey mantle and crazy
legs hirsh and maurice rocket richard were my heroes, a
boy's got to have heroes. and sports taught me to dance.
i say that sports are dance. often aggressive nasty ass in-
your-face macho dance, of course, but dance, nonetheless.

thus, i ponder my youth as i limp slowly
along thru the hills.

a breeze shakes the poplar leaves.
they make a paper-like rattling sound.

stella eats grass along the side of the road.
the gravel crunches loudly underneath my boots.

i'm 73 now

and each moment

is better than the last.

feeling lucky?

jesus, i just heard that cassidy has covid.
so does my friend jeff in new prague.
al and laura and their kid have the virus.
a bunch of birdie's cousins in mexico
got it too.

wisconsin, minnesota, iowa, and the dakotas are
all hot spots, solid red on the national covid maps.
and a bunch of kids over at durand high school
have tested positive, not sure they're in quarantine tho,
that part of the county either shy on brain power
or big on denial - or both

everyone's saying it's going to be a long winter.
osterholm described it as a "winter of covid hell".
fauci said "it's time to double down".
there could be half a million deaths before all this is over.
i say run for the hills...

in olympia, tennesee, in 1876 it rained meat.
that's right, little pieces of meat rained from the skies.
no one ever figured that one out.

on the other hand, in 1945, tsutomu yamaguchi survived
both the atomic bomb in hiroshima and the atomic bomb in
nagasaki. either he was lucky or unlucky or both.

and in 1972, enraged by extreme heat and hunger, the ele-
phants of chandaka forest in india stampeded and killed 24
people. the elephant god, ganesh, of course, is the god of
wisdom, and the remover of all obstacles.

none of this stuff fits in my small human brain.

three more non-haiku

thunder rolling in
rain drips off gutters
my hands are growing old

~

chocolate ice cream melting
watching the blue moon rise
let's walk home

~

war plods on in ukraine
is it spring there too?
apple blossoms float away

groans to a stop

and now i am worried how my grandkids
will survive this world, how they will navigate
the cops, the dictator wannabe, the plague.
i can see minnesota from here, across the lake,
i wonder how life is with them in minnesota,
i wonder what living well means when thick,
dull, white cops kneel on the necks of descendants
of black slaves, kneel on their necks until
they can't breathe, kneel on them until they die
the very slow death that happens so fast.

and we are spinning in circles backwards now,
we are spinning in circles. we are less than what
we were, we are no longer people, not now,
we are no longer people, we are thugs now at best,
we are animals at best, we have become criminals
and we live criminal lives, we are now the sound
a great machine makes as it groans and groans
and groans to a stop.

good art

"good art smells like life."
            - jim harrison

susan wants me to take up the floorboards
beneath the sink to see if there's a mouse
dead down there. i'm not sure i want to
bother, not picking up much of a smell, why
pull everything apart?

on the other hand, i can't really smell that much,
burned out my sense of smell working in the trades
all those years, sealing walls with shellacs, burning
off old layers of paint, the stuff with lead in it.
probably, my lungs took a beating day after day,
i figure my nose did too.

and on the other other hand, i can smell good art
from bad at 1000 yards.

no, really.

la frontera

(for federico)

so, ok, if my darkening hands
now match the darkening skies,
if the waves raging in from the lake turn
and head south towards wabasha and
reeds landing, towards minnesota,
will i settle into the drunken life of
olives and basil and an almost new skin?

and will that skin be the thickness of a
stillborn angel (if angels, in fact, can be stillborn)?
will it turn and face the answers flooding in from the west,
will it embrace feet so tired that they cannot sing,
cannot fight the good fight, cannot track their way thru
the siberian woods into the moonlight?

and if i cannot walk any kind of straight line,
or dance any kind of long, slow, awkward dance,
will you or your sister, will your mother,
will that aunt that always got drunk at xmas,
will any of you then, please, take me back
into the fold, into the ministry, into the village?
and will i finally have that chance to grow old,
the one i lost out on last time around?

please, please straighten my hair, mi amiga,
straighten my tie, straighten me into some form
of understanding here, beg me to come back
to your house again, to join you for an evening
of wine and bread and song and prayers,
for the old stories, the ones from back in the day,

from when we used to mow the lawn into a fort,
a maze, a wandering place, a palace.

and please, please will you finally take me back
to the front lines, to la frontera, to the actual border
when i have no will left inside my hands, my knees,
when i cannot think straight or see straight or be straight,
or even challenge what is said today and also tomorrow,
when all is wrongheaded and weak and wanting?

shuffleboard

so, i spent two or three years of my life in nursing homes,
helping the old and infirm walk to the bathroom, wash-
ing them, cleaning off their privates, getting them their
dinners, helping them eat, reading to them and now the
tables have been turned and here i am being washed and
clothed and fed and needing help to get to the bathroom
and i don't really like this much, i vastly preferred being
the cowboy sort, running around like a madman, doing
this that and the other, riding off in every which direction,
throwing spaghetti against the wall, bouncing off said
walls and honkin' getting things done pronto and now i'm
up against it, ain't i? i'm the man at seventy-three facing
the end, or maybe the beginning of the end, or maybe the
end of the middle, but not the middle of the middle any-
more, facing my own shortening road, and not liking it,
cause all i wanna do is hit it hard still, like forever rock-
ing, but realizing that that probably ain't gonna happen
so much anymore, cause we all drive off the road into the
brush sooner or later, we all take that dive into the ditch,
even gurdjieff and his disciples, the ones hustling hard and
painting sparrows yellow and selling them as carnaries
in the marketplace in i think it was tashkent back in the
nineteen-twenties just to eat, even they had to settle in,
eventually, for shuffleboard and long, slow games of chess
at the park all summer long.

when the poem comes

when the poem comes
you gotta get it down fast.
or at least get a shot off at it.
otherwise, it's gone
and yr watching the white tail
of that big buck
disappearing into the underbrush
down some coulee ravine
off of back valley road.

there are rabbits everywhere this morning

(also for jim denomie)

there are rabbits everywhere this morning.
the grass is way beyond green, the leaves are
so lovely green beyond green beyond green.
every square inch of sky is filled with birdsong.
every square inch of sky is o god so blue.
oh, and by the way, the cities are burning.

and now a rabbit, long ears and all, wanders
up to me in my chair here in the backyard,
hops across trent's yard and watches me.
i call for susan to come look, but the rabbit
disappears into the green-ness, into the grass,
into the morning, into the green-ness morning.
oh, and by the way, the cities are burning.

and the breeze comes up and it's a perfect morning
and i am in love with life cause susan is here again
and we had a wonderful breakfast in the backyard
and my back isn't hurting much. so i sit and write
and soon i will meditate and then work in the garden,
maybe help the vines grow up that back wall, and
later on we'll take the dog for a walk by the river.
and, oh, by the way, the cities are burning.

the cicada

the cicada doesn't bother with labels,
doesn't bother with a mission statement.
it merely waits seven years,
shows up above ground,
and grinds its music
into daily ecstatic oblivion.

i say god bless their little insect hearts,
god bless their strange and remorseless mission.

and see you in seven years.

the nest

rumi sez:

"sufis know that grace comes
when something is taken away".

dougie sez:

"the grave
you will be buried in
is a nest.

prepare for death
the same
as you would
bring new life
into this
world."

the water lilies

the white water lilies blossom in the ditches between
nelson and alma each spring, thousands of them.

i am trying to understand each and every note yusef
lateef ever played, in each song, on every album.

i love to watch my wife sleep on the couch with the dog,
each wrapped around the other, the dog snoring hard.

if i could get back to the chicago institute of art someday,
i would sit with chagall's stained glass windows forever.

considering han shan and the devil track river

i've never been down the devil track
up in northern minnesota,
never kayaked it,
never even seen it.
maybe this summer, once the virus is gone,
or at least quieted down,
i'll get there.

of course, i've been close, been
out of grand marais to a pretty nice bar
up the gunflint trail, but that's
all pretty much gringo stuff,
i'm older now and soft and
i get around mostly with my wife
in her small honda sedan.

plus, the closest i've come to han shan's cave
is probably when i carried snyder's
translation of the cold mountain poems,
backpack roaming amerika,
hitchhiking thru the sixties.
although, lenfesty was over here
the other night with flora for tea
and he told us tales of his pilgrimage
to china, of the cave, of han shan.

on the other hand, in india i made love
to an italian, a german, and an australian
all in the same week.
well, that's a lie.
(i seem to lie alot).
the australian was almost a month later,

right before i came down with hep,
the night before sona and her posse
showed up from the south,
kerala state i think, still high from drinking
cobra venom, high enough to see god,
smart enough to not o.d. and die.

but, back to northern minnesota.
it seems you gotta climb and portage alot
to make it down the devil track river.
not sure i'm up to that physically,
seventy-one and all.
more likely i'll sit at its mouth, the spot
where it pours into superior,
ponder whether the devil pools there,
whether i can feel his essence,
the sulphur, the groans, the fear.
and right then and there
where the devil unleashes
into the big lake, i will sit and
listen to the river pound its body
hard against the rocks,

watch

the river disappearing

forever.

fish taco

i'm eating susan's freshly made lefse which is pretty much
exactly like the lefse my mom dagny used to make back in
st. louis park and also my norske grandma selmine made
back in winona in the fifties, transcendent thin palaces
of lightly fried mashed and rolled out potatoes, topped
with a layer of butter, curled in my hand, downed in three
bites, then off to the kitchen to beg for more. sometimes,
if i was lucky, they came with a sprinkling of sugar, say if it
was a holiday like christmas or maybe the 4th of july and
we were out parked on a sandbar on the river on uncle
don's houseboat for the weekend. on the other hand, i
am trying to remember my uncle alfredo's tortillas, but
i don't, instead i remember his salsas, each fresh and
particular to that moment's meal, something red with
tomatoes for tacos de pollo and something green for his
pork tamales. and, yes, i especially remember the turkey
he cooked once, shot up with red wine for days with a
hypodermic needle and it ended up tasting like the best
ham ever as we feasted together and shot off shotguns
in the front yard that night (to announce my arrival) and
drank all night till the high desert chihuahuan dawn and
then i begged to go back to the hotel to sleep, cause i was
kinda a wimp about such things and was dead on my feet.
no, for the greatest tortilla ever i would have to focus on
the one that wrapped the greatest fish taco ever, which, of
course, was probably maybe perhaps from that stand in
east l.a., the spot that i found long ago wandering on foot
like forever across l.a. from my nephew peter's apartment
thru los feliz and then silver lake and then on across into
echo park (did i even make it to echo park?) and god,
there it was on a corner on whittier boulevard, and it was
so praise god good that i ordered two and downed them
fast and then two more and they were so cheap and good

that i went back to the counter and thanked those folks pro-
fusely and paid them again, paid them a second time, cause
such great and worthy noble efforts deserve gratitude, a great
taco stand just exactly what heaven on earth is all about my
friends, i say god bless all great taco stands forever and ever
and ever amen.

if everyone is a yoga teacher, who grows the food?

(also for gary snyder)

if everyone is a yoga teacher,
who grows the food?

if everyone is a massage therapist,
who fixes the engine on the truck?

if everyone is an online life coach,
who cares for our daughters after surgery?

if everyone is a reiki master,
who gets the trash to the dump?

chop wood, carry water.

danger

now a huge brown and white immature eagle
picks at carrion in front of the studio
out on 2nd street.

with each bite it looks up for danger.
i am a good ways away, in the backyard,
mostly hidden by oversize fiddlehead ferns.

but i know how the eagle feels:
trump, pandemic, putin, bad cops,
small town minds, a bad football team,
the war in ukraine, climate change...
the list seems endless.

and me?

with each bite of life,
i too look up for danger.

i sleep under a bear skin sometimes

i sleep under a bear skin sometimes,
the one on the studio bed downriver,
the one that lenfestey gave me, the one
that turned my dreams into late night
b-movies, all of us lost and gone in wave
after wave of junior high '60's delusion:
bardot, hemmingway, willie mays,
steve mcqueen...

and yes, sometimes that bear skin deepens
under me, sleeps holding me in its arms,
its immense paws. and then and only then,
we sleep together the deep sleep, the long
sleep, the sleep of winters and even years,
or maybe it's minutes or hours,
or god knows how long,

that same black bear back today
wandering thru this now
empty town,
that same bear
wondering where all the humans went,
how they all disappeared
so quickly

and why summers
have grown so long.

six lines for kurt vonnegut

outside, under the magnificently leafed sugar maple,

longing for the insidious black flies to find other work,

i put on a light, but long-sleeved shirt for protection.

it's cool, almost cold, tho mid-august here in the north

and i find it interesting that my hands do not match,

fascinating that the clouds have no lasting home in the sky.

and then it was suddenly gone

there is the sweetness of birdsong
in the air here this morning.
and that same woodpecker
goes off again over by the river,
for maybe the tenth time.

and now i know we'll make it
thru this plague,
we'll make it thru this virus,
although we are now gonna be known
as the covid 19 generation.

there is not much poetry to that name,
unlike the "spanish flu" after world war 1,
the "black death" of the 14th century,
or the "yellow fever" of 1693 in philadelphia,
where the good citizens of the "city of brotherly love"
thought that their slaves were immune to the disease
and thus should be their nurses.

and of course they weren't.
and thus, everybody died,
both black and white,
until a hard frost came in the fall
and killed the mosquitoes
that carried that deadly disease.

then it was suddenly gone
and everyone turned and
went about the business
of living again,

that business of living

much more prosperous,
of course,

for some
than others.

after germany

1.

since the trip to germany over the summer,
i'm really digging
on mad king ludwig of bavaria,
the creator of disneylandesque castles,
me a fan of most "more is more" types,
types like ludwig,
sun ra and his arkestra,
howard finster,
most 2nd graders with crayons,
and the whole entire notion of mayflies.

i also want to mention diane di prima here.
read a poem by her today,
remember her, the beat poet?
i think she was one of the best,
in my humble opinion only behind
snyder and ginsberg.
sure, michael mclure had his moments,
ferlinghetti certainly is good.
some would vote for kerouac or corso.
i like di prima.

2.

tourists walk by and get into their audis.
they drive off back to the homes in the suburbs.

me, i miss friedrichshaffen,
i miss the bodensee, felicia, allain,
the garden at the waldenhorn.
i would like to spend more time there some day,

there and in the rather craggy alps,
the german alps,
the swiss alps,
italian alps,
the alps in austria.
at this very moment,
i am obsessed with alps.

3.

i feel a breeze,
the leaves start singing,
off in the background
slowly, in both long and short tones,
some kinda postmodern mash-up
of bach and the duluth band low.
stella finds a spot in the shade to sit and wait.
but wait for what?

sometimes when i'm out in the woods
my senses seem to cross,
like when i see tree bark,
especially thick bark,
say like a cottonwood has,
when i see it with my eyes,

it's more like a feeling,
a feeling inside my body,
where i feel with my tongue,
only in my belly,

almost a taste.

a short note for ferlinghetti

so, verne left a couple of weeks ago,
richard knopf died last week.
chris and aldo and charlie passed
over in the last few months.
dad's been gone 28 years now.

i can't even remember when
grandma was last with us.

and yes, my hands have become translucent,
i look at them and they fly suddenly across the room
across the lake across the country, down into mexico,
into chihuahua, and ventura is still alive pilar is still alive
lupe is still alive consuelo is still alive alfredo is still alive.
alfredo is still cooking that turkey that he injected with
wine to make it taste like the best ham ever in the universe.
and now i have a broken leg in a cast up to my hip,
i'm on crutches, ventura has taken me to a strip club in
juarez and now we've left and we're looking for the car and
he's wandered off to see a friend, even though it is three
in the morning and it's a damn tough side of town and my
spanish sucks and i couldn't run away from a duck if i was
in trouble.

and now i am back at that club at 26th and 26th, what was
it called? i'm watching the wallets, the suburbs, sun ra and
the archestra, and now i'm outside the club watching
grandmaster flash and the furious five get off the bus, and
now it's the fillmore west in '68 and i'm 15 feet from
hendrix and i figure out that he's playing left-handed and
that his strings are strung upside down and now i'm with
tom of taurus up north of the city in marin somewhere,

we're digging on the incredible string band, oh they were so lovely, all of them, all so filled with light.

and god, ferlinghetti died this week.

personally, i loved the guy, i don't really care what you think, popular poets pay a price for the joy they put into their work. if a bomb took out all the academic poets in the country i'm not sure i would worry much.

holes

inside the wall there are holes.
inside the holes there are walls.

we live in these walls sometimes.
sometimes we live in the holes.

russia invades ukraine.

paradise

smelling
the loveliest pink rose ever

the riots in the city
disappear

and for just a minute
i know paradise

again.

across the river

1.

across the river from poona, across the mula mutha, i am sitting on the rooftop enjoying a respite from the rains and watching my neighbor three floors below chopping wood. he is of the lowest caste, a dalit. his clothes are rags and i notice that his axe is so dull that the blade doesn't really enter the wood with each glancing blow. it's more like he is simply pounding away at the wood, trying some- how, magically, to split it in two. most likely he cannot afford the price of a sharpening file. anyways, a file would only wear away the steel of the axe, wear it away down to little or nothing some day. and axes are not cheap and he must chop wood for the cremation fires to be able to feed his family and that is not an easy job.

2.

and now i hear music, someone is playing a shinai out- side, playing like coltrane meets ravi shankar only pretty stoned, and someone else is playing a big drum and i look out over the parking lot in front of the building and there are two men in dilapidated military uniforms there and between them their companion is a dancing bear.

but the bear does not seem happy today, tho he is dancing anyway, but it is not a happy dance. the bear has a chain around its leg and it cannot move far. besides its hair is molting and that makes it look old, older than it probably is, makes it look sad, half-naked sad.

so, tho i am kinda weak, i make my way down the stairs and put a few rupees in the tin at one of the men's feet. i don't have much to give, i have been sick and in india too long now and i am broke and, eventually, i will need to get a ticket home somehow. perhaps my money will help him feed the bear better today. one can only hope.

3.

and this morning i feel sicker than yesterday morning. the hepatitis is getting the best of me, i am wasted, i cannot find my body, i'm not sure i have a body, there is only this thinking, this watching, although something seems to be lying on this thin mattress on the floor, perhaps that thing is my body, hard to tell.

and then the racket starts up again and my frayed nerves jolt into reaction, a scratchy, fuckin' loudspeaker from the alley building behind me blaring away another sugary indian pop song. and then, suddenly, a second speaker from a house in front of where i lay starts blasting out a different sugary pop song and they smash against each other exactly right there in my lying on the rooftop sick out of my body mind, my wants to self-destruct from this aural chaos mind, my o god i need some peace and quiet this morning mind, but this is india and i'm lost in bed now fifty plus days and turning the volume down on life a bit would be nice today, but i see that's not gonna happen because, frankly, my neighbors love the blare of all this, different strokes for different folks, i guess.

and once more i must let go, let go of my senses, let go of my mind, of my body, of my family back home, let go of my life, let go of awakening, let go of everything, sink into this great river always moving life sounds sights smells river, always bombarded, constantly moving, always, always...

and swamiji, isn't that the reason you came to india in the first place?

4.

later on, when the rains break, i hear a band, i hear marching band music coming up from up the street here alongside the river. the music is drifting my way and so i get out of bed and make my way across the rooftop to the railing where i am living on a stair top landing and sure enough there is a band now outside my building and they are dressed in ragged marching band uniforms, holes in the knees, holes in the elbows and their music seems to have holes in it also and i can't tell what they are playing tho i am enjoying it immensely as i have always adored the ragged elbows and knees of indian street music and this is certainly about as street as you can get here in india, in maharashtra, here in poona, in yerawada, and it's all coming to me now, i'm digging this music but what song are they playing? what song are they playing? it sounds so familiar, but my mind can't quite get around the melody, can't quite grok it, they are bending all or most of the notes indian stylee bending them all over the place, bending everything in sight, everything in the world that will not break, every note, every child, every tree, every building, and even the river and trucks on the street are bending now and then suddenly it comes to me like sun suddenly shining thru the clouds, they are playing

"when the saints come marching in"

and i have a moment of realization and absolute delight, of joy, and now new orleans and india have suddenly fused in a crazy, amazing jazz-like musical moment and yes, this is fucking why god invented music and india and new orleans in the first place! this is why!

on carpel tunnel #2

how to write a poem each and every morning
when my wrists are filled with angry snails
tracing an acidic slime across skin
and muscle and down
into bone?

chaos theory #2

ok, if a butterfly in new jersey floats gently west and then
north for awhile, if it settles in on a tree limb, say a blaze
red rust orange sugar maple in a wisconsin autumn, if it
sits and rests, does russia suddenly apologize and leave
ukraine not only overnight, but in a heartbeat?

if toni morrison re-enters this picture and reads from
Sula, even this late at night, after pretty much each and
every one of us has turned out the lights and gone to bed
and said our prayers and tried to get our spiritual house
in order, does trump realize his wrong-headedness, his
ego that won't quit, his insanities, does he then deflate his
propaganda machine and funnel all its funds to "save the
children"?

and if the coywolf i thought i saw driving from fargo
to st. cloud and then south to northfield a few weeks back
quietly develops a taste for fine dining, say seared scallops
in a light butter and garlic sauce, with new potatoes and
asparagus and a nice inexpensive, but quality pinot gri-
gio, does africa (and by africa i mean senegal or ghana or
nigeria or maybe even egypt) then win the world cup and
consequently provide enough clean water and ample food
to the good folks locked in its slums, does it then open the
doors to its political prisons and in shame and regret let
souls run free?

i say yes.

for susan

i thought i would write a love poem
for susan today.
i'll keep it short, cause
love poems are hard.

there'll be something about birds,
she loves birds.
i'll mention her dog
and how she takes it for long walks daily.
and how she talks forever to stella
when nobody's listening, talks
in long paragraphs, rambling on
and on.

and her gardening, god the woman
can garden. i'll mention how the back yard
is gorgeous again, how her purple garden
is always the best. i'll mention how much
i love her hostas.

more likely tho, the poem will stumble
around in circles til it falls
near the door
and lays sprawled there
for months.

it is beyond difficult to describe beauty.
it is near impossible to describe love.

the begonias

and now there are rocks everywhere,
rocks hard on our bare feet.
and there is shouting everywhere now.
there is a singing that is almost silence,
and i am passing my mind thru that silence,
i am passing my hands thru singing that
is silence.

and now we are escaping the virus,
escaping the cities, escaping the wars against
the people. we are escaping time and its antecedents,
we are sitting here together now, waiting for dante,
for bosch, for bruegel, waiting for the dark
times to end, to end again and again.

but i will remember when the moment turned,
(as moments always do), that dragging moment
that turned and then spring came, or a kind of spring,
came strong and fast, and the very gentle begonias,
the very bright yellow begonias,

pushed the sun thru to our eyes,
pushed our eyes thru to worlds beyond our eyes,
and pushed on thru to worlds beyond that.
and then we could all finally at last
breathe once more praise god, we
could breathe once more
we could all breathe once more at last.

and the begonias, the very gentle begonias
the very bright yellow begonias
came strong and fast

and this place became our home again
and the whole world were heroes.
and we were the whole world.

"In Dzogchen practice the beginning and the end are not seen as separate. The very starting point is the end itself. There is no difference between the alpha and omega, in the sense that when you realize Dzogchen, you have not realized anything different from what you already possess."

- Traleg Kyabgon Rinpoche

www.ingramcontent.com/pod-product-compliance
Lightning Source LLC
Chambersburg PA
CBHW022156080426
42734CB00006B/460